The Hope Cove Area during The Second World War 1939-45

Arthur L. Clamp

Four recollections of the wartime years of this area with personnel from R.A.F. Bolt Head and the radar station on Bolberry Down.

This version of the book is virtually as originally published.
There are now additional pages at the back providing information about the author.

The republishing project is being managed by Arthur's grandson, Steven Gibson. We aim to find all the research that he was involved in publishing, preserving it for the next generation as part of 'The Clamp Collection'.

Introduction

The present delightful coastal area around Hope Cove belies the important and part secret role it played between the years 1940 to 1945 when an advanced fighter plane base was in operation here supported by two secret radar installations. Any visitor to this area of South Devon could not be blamed for thinking that the quiet and serene countryside has been like this for many years attracting people to its beautiful cliffs, small villages and numerous creeks.

This was far from the situation in the dark years of the Second World War when England was threatened by air and by sea and when both opponents were secretly developing radar techniques in air navigation and plane identification and attack procedures.

This very southern area of the U.K. lent itself to being used as a base area from which operations could be mounted, planes flown without using up precious fuel from inland airfields and a radar watchful eye kept on the German's own radar system known to be operating along most of the French coast.

Supporting the airfield at R.A.F. Bolt Head and the two radar installations, one by the airfield and the other on Bolberry Down one section being very close to the cliffs, were wireless stations on Pinhey Hill and at Preston Farm, a searchlight unit at Burleigh Farm and various gun emplacements along the coastline.

This assembly of military units required many hundreds of R.A.F., W.A.A.F. and Army personnel to run them and these in turn required accommodation in the requisitioned hotels in the area, in houses and farms and on the stations and in nissen huts erected at the gun sites.

For just five years this area changed completely in character and people living here with many additional military people visiting the radar installations and noting the secret developments taking place. Such an area soon attracted the attention of the enemy and from time to time attacks took place, allied planes often taking to the skies for defence and also for air sea rescue missions up and down the Channel.

This illustrated booklet can only record a small part of those turbulent and uncertain days but it is hoped that this in itself will be better than nothing. The booklet shows just one chapter in the changing years in this area.

Arthur L. Clamp
April, 1992

Acknowledgements

I must record my warm thanks for the time and effort many people spent in relating their experiences during the war years and for their letters, information and photographs shown in this booklet.

Much enthusiasm was given for this undertaking in getting together some kind of record of events which took place in the Hope Cove area from 1941 to 1945 however incomplete it may be.

First I thank Mr. Owen Masters at Hope Cove for suggesting in 1991 that this would be "a good thing to do" as he had gathered some names of visitors enquiring about their years they spent here and then to the following people for lots of memories, letters, interviews, sketches and photographs:
Mrs. B. Stone, B. Coombs, Miss D. Prowse, J. Rossiter, Mrs. P. McNichol, J. Stribling, B. Rossiter, Mrs. J. Smith (Fry), Mrs. F. Pilditch, Miss O. J. Smith, H. Child, V. H. White, L. F. Trew, and to the staff at R.A.F. Hendon, North London and the Public Record Office, London.

In a booklet of this size it is simply not possible to include all the events of those changing and turbulent years with the coming and goings of many hundreds of military personnel in this area of Devon. I hope, however, it will be something of a reminder of those now far off days and an acknowledgement of the lives, time and energy given towards winning the Second World War by many people.

Two Remaining Buildings from the Second World War

On the left is the brick and concrete operations room of the wireless station on Pinhey's Hill and, on the right, one of the buildings housing part of the searchlight unit at Burleigh Farm now used as a dairy.

1. Sewage disposal works.
2. Fuel compound, post and wire.
3. Sergeant's quarters, nissen.
4. Sergeant's quarters, nissen.
5. Sergeant's quarters, nissen.
6. Sergeant's ablutions, concrete block and timber.
7. Sergeant's mess, nissen.
8. Ration store, hand craft.
9. Barrack hut, timber.
10. 20,000 gallon static tank, brick construction.
11. 24,000 gallon water storage tower and tank.
12. Trailer pump house, concrete block.
13. Barrack hut, timber.
14. Dining room for 200, nissen.
15. Barrack hut, timber.
16. Guardroom, concrete block.
17. Station armoury, nissen.
18. A.M.W.D. store, timber and corrugated iron.
19. A.M.W.D. rest hut and store, hand craft.
20. A.M.W.D. store, timber and corrugated iron.
21. A.M.W.D. store, timber and corrugated iron.
22. A.M.W.D. workshop and store, plaster board.
23. A.M.W.D. store, timber and corrugated iron.
24. A.M.W.D. fitters shop, nissen.
25. 24,000 gallon aviation petrol installation.
26. S.A.A. stores, type B, nissen.
27. Over enlarged blister hangar.
28. Station headquarters, seco hutting.
29. Equipment store, seco hutting.
30. Technical latrine, concrete and block.
31. M.T. office and rest room, seco hutting.
32. Two stores, concrete and block.
33. Over enlarged blister hangar.
34. M.T. W.A.A.F. rest room, nissen.
35. M.T. store, beach hutting.
36. Bar and rod track aircraft parking areas.
37. Lubricants, and inflammable store.
38. Projector room, nissen.
39. Flight office, nissen.
40. Flight C.O.s office, timber.
41. R.A.F. latrine, concrete block.
42. Bulk oil compound, post and wire.
43. Four barrack huts, nissen.
44. R.A.F. latrine, concrete and block.
45. Equipment store, packing case.
46. W.A.A.F. latrine, concrete and block.
47. Gas clothing store, nissen.
48. Requisitioned civilian houses.

R.A.F. Bolt Head Airfield

This advanced landing ground for fighter operations was the largest wartime site in the Hope Cove area coming into use on 18th December, 1941, and reverting to a care and maintenance role on 25th April, 1945, finally closing in 1947.

It was at its peak in the first half of 1944 when giving support to the Normandy landings on 6th June 1944; much of the construction of the airfield taking place during 1942. The above sketch map shows most of the buildings and aircraft waiting areas. The sketch map on the cover of this book gives an overall view including the two runways covered with metal grids.

Close by was R.A.F. Hope Cove, a radar installation, which worked very closely with Squadrons using the airfield and with the help of Polish crews flying from here developed many radar detection and navigation techniques in 1941/2 which played a large part in the success of the thrust into France in 1944. Because of the secret nature of this work many of the achievements and technical developments, more than matching the German's radar networks, have gone largely unrecorded and will probably never have their full acknowledgements included in books about this war.

This small grass twin runway airfield was brought into operation as it provided facilities for aircraft to operate at their maximum flying range over enemy territory being at the edge of the coastline in this part of Devon, the second southernmost area of England.

It did not initially have many of the facilities of a normal active airfield but came under the control of Exeter and allowed planes to fly out over the channel within seconds of taking off and, in many later instances, gave refuge to planes returning from sorties and raids who were either running out of fuel or damaged to the extent that they just managed to reach the safety of England's coastline.

The first aircraft to use this airfield were Lysanders of No. 16 Squadron engaged in chemical warfare exercises over the Channel, then by two more Lysanders from 276 Squadron, Air Sea Rescue.

However, it was the Polish 317 Squadron who were pressing the authorities to allow them to go into action as soon as possible and were quietly flying sorties into France and working close with the radar developments at R.A.F. Hope Cove G.C.I. station.

During 1942 the station grew in size and extent. Barrack huts, flights and administration offices were built close to the aircraft parking areas and a bulk fuel storage and enlarged blister hangars were also completed.

Two runways were laid with metal grids and later extended with bar and rod tracking, used also for accessing aircraft to their parking areas.

By now Bolt Head station could support a resident squadron of fighters with accommodation and messes on the station and further accommodation in Hope Cove with an officers' mess in the Cottage Hotel. The airfield was upgraded to a satellite station.

Activities increased with the arrival of Canadians of 402 Squadron assisting with Royal Navy escort duties and convoy patrols and in April, 1941, three Polish Squadrons of the Exeter Wing extended the stations use, these being 306, 308 and 302 escorting Boston bombers on a raid to Morlaix, France.

In April, 1942, five Messerschmitt planes attacked the station (see entry on page 8) but not a lot of damage was sustained. Czech pilots were now operating from here, then came 257 Squadron with Typhoons in September followed by 610 Squadron (County of Chester) aircraft and a further attack by German planes this time by eight Focke Wulf 190s dropping bombs but not hitting any buildings. The year ended with several more hit and run raids and the station was now operating round the clock with many visiting planes and personnel flying in for very short periods of stay bringing visitors as well to see the secret work taking place at R.A.F. Hope Cove G.C.I. station.

By the opening months of 1943 an impressive number of Fighter Squadrons had used this small airfield, these being 302, 306, 308, 307, 310, 257, 133, 401, 412, 610, 234 and 266, a good indication of the amount of activity taking place here which also included many air sea rescues. An unpredicted use was when planes returned from missions over France and were damaged, or were running very low on fuel or were lost through bad weather coming in unexpectedly. Many a pilot landed safely here, while others partly crashed landed to safety. Unfortunately some also crashed into the cliffs along this coastline killing pilots and crew.

Many of the Fighter Squadrons used Spitfires which were mainly employed to escort bombers on raids well into France. They often joined with Spitfires from more inland stations and would number in all 30-40 planes on a mission raid. These escorting duties with occasional air sea rescue work was much the order of the day throughout 1943 but there were days when cloud levels came down and flying ceased for awhile giving, no doubt, some restful hours for crews down in Hope Cove or on stand by on the station.

Many of the raids into enemy occupied areas were coded as *Rhubarb, Circus, Rodeo*, etc., and these are explained on page 17. It was these duties which occupied the Squadrons for much of their time here. In 1943 R.A.F. Bolt Head came under the control of R.A.F. Harrowbeer, a station just to the north of Plymouth which also had Fighter Squadrons.

One example of a *Rhubarb* was an attack by twelve Bostons of 88 Squadron on St. Malo, France, during July, 1943. Bombers used Exeter and escort was provided by Ibsley, Portreath and other stations, with two Squadrons from Bolt Head making some 100 aircraft in all. They flew low level until about 30 miles from the French coast to avoid being detected by German radar, then climbed to 8,000 ft. bombing and turning back for Start Point before descending to sea level where radar operators on Bolberry Down or at the G.C.I. station could assist should clouds descend or warn of any following enemy fighter planes. The planes provided close escort for the bombers and also undertook surveillance duties over German airfields in France.

In September, 1943, 610 Squadron from Perranporth came here for *Rhubarbs* and were successful in downing four Messerschmitt Bf110s during a spell of duty. At this time the more powerful Spitfire XII was coming into use and a few of these were operational from here into 1944.

This crucial year for Allied Forces put all stations on their maximum operational basis leading to the eventful D-Day landings in France on 6th June, 1944, the beginning of the end for Germany's occupation of Europe.

The two nearby radar stations had made very worthwhile contributions in assisting allied aircraft to pin point the position of an enemy plane and give details of its height, speed, and wind speeds and direction, prior to going into an attack, this approach had reduced enemy air power quite significantly during the landings.

R.A.F. Bolt Head was mainly used for escort duties on the large amount of shipping building up for the assault. In April, 1944, 41 Squadron came here with the powerful Spitfire XIIs. Aircraft from 275, 276, 610, 263 and 151 Squadrons came here for short spells of duty as well and a constant surveillance programme was followed over France where it was thought German troops would be assembling to defend the French coastline.

However, there were moments of relaxation at the local dances and film shows on camp and in the barn at Hope Cove. Also it is recorded on 18th September, 1944, the perimeter fence was being repaired to prevent repeated invasions of pigs! It was not always all work. Time off could be spent in nearby Kingsbridge and some lengths of the coastline could be walked along.

The successful landings by Allied Forces in France and their inland thrust would sooner rather than later mean that the role R.A.F. Bolt Head had played for three years would diminish. On D-Day itself there was only 41 Squadron here providing cover for Typhoons from R.A.F. Harrowbeer both Squadrons of planes attacking targets in the Channel Islands. 41 Squadron was replaced by 263 staying for three weeks then came 275 air sea rescue Squadron operating with Walrus, Spitfire and Defiant planes.

Reconnaissance flights over France were deployed trying to pin point V1 rocket sites and bombing raids aimed at fuel dumps, railways, roads and bridges in an effort to slow down the retreating German armies. Escort duties were provided by fighter planes from Bolt Head for many of these operations.

By the autumn of 1944 the station was out of full use, the theatre of war having moved well into France. 151 Squadron occasionally used the airfield and in October, 1944, another instance of aircraft running out of fuel occurred, this time two Spitfires landing in the nick of time.

There were many celebration parties in the early months of 1945 (see page 8) and the base was reduced to a care and maintenance use on 25th April, 1945, thus bringing a changing and exciting wartime use to an end.

Very occasionally a plane would land here as did a Wellington in May, 1946 and a variety of practice interceptions took place by 691 Squadron. By 1947 all activities ceased and much of the site reverted to farmland.

Sea Rescue off Devon Coast

Air and sea rescue operations took place from time to time when pilots were able to radio in either returning in an aircraft seriously damaged in a raid or, more often, when fuel ran out. Here Squadron Leader Sagjinski alights from a rescue craft thought to be in the Torbay area, together with a colleague.

On Stand By

Aircrews and ground staff maintained a twenty-four hour watch at R.A.F. Bolt Head and were ready to be scrambled at a moments notice. Here officers are outside of one of the billets on the station but none have been identified.

Squadron Leader Sagjinski

One of the many polish officers who flew from R.A.F. Bolt Head airfield probably with 317 Squadron which was one of the first to fly from the small airfield in 1941-2. He proudly stands by his Austin Seven at the Esso petrol pump behind Grand View Hotel, Outer Hope.

550/A PILOT P/O PURVIS (CAPTAIN) F/E SGT LEARY
B/A F/SGT SCHOLEFIELD NAVIGATOR SGT STODDART.
WOP/AIR SGT GUTHRIE M/U/G SGT WRIGHT
R/G SGT SCOBLE.

BORDEAUX AUGUST 12TH 1944.

AT 1123 HRS ON AUGUST 12 550/A TOOK OFF TO BOMB THE OIL STORAGE ADJACENT TO THE SUBMARINE PENS AT BORDEAUX. ALL WENT WELL UNTIL THE BOMB DOORS WERE OPENED ON THE BOMBING RUN WHEN AT 10000 FT 'A' WAS HIT BY FLAK, THE PORT OUTER CAUGHT FIRE AND WAS FEATHERED, THE HYDRAULIC GEAR AND BOTH ASI WERE RENDERED U/S. THE FAILURE OF THE ELECTRICAL CIRCUIT MADE IT IMPOSSIBLE TO RELEASE THE BOMBS. THE F/E (SGT LEARY) WAS WOUNDED IN THE LEG AND ARM AND ALSO THE B/A (F/SGT SCHOLEFIELD) SLIGHTLY IN THE HAND. A SECOND BURST OF FLAK RENDERED THE STBD INNER ENGINE U/S DUE TO AN OIL LEAK, THIS ENGINE ALSO WAS FEATHERED. OTHER DAMAGE SUSTAINED WAS RUDDER AND AILERON (TRIMMERS SHOT AWAY), THROTTLE AND REV. CONTROLS TO STBD OUTER SEVERED, AND THE TRAILING AERIAL RENDERED U/S - IN CONSEQUENCE OF THIS 'A' WAS RENDERED TEMPORARILY OUT OF CONTROL AND LOST HEIGHT TO 1500 FT, WHEN THE PILOT GAINED CONTROL AND WITH DIFFICULTY HEADED 'A' FOR HOME, BOMBS BEING JETTISONED ONE BY ONE FROM 4610N-0215W FROM 1500 FT ALSO THE REAR GUNS ONE M/U/G AND BOTH FRONT GUNS AND ALL AMMUNITION PLUS THE ELSAN IN ORDER TO GAIN HEIGHT, BUT THE PILOT HAD GREAT DIFFICULTY IN KEEPING TO 1500 FT. THE NAVIGATOR (SGT STODDART) ASSISTED BY THE W/OP (SGT GUTHRIE) DRESSED THE F/ENGINEERS WOUNDS AND MADE HIM AS COMFORTABLE AS POSSIBLE. ALL THE CREW SPEAK WITH PRAISE OF THE PERFORMANCE PUT UP BY THE F/ENGINEER WHO ALTHOUGH IN GREAT PAIN GAVE DIRECTIONS TO THE PILOT WHO WAS NURSING 'A' ALONG ON 2 ENGINES, REGARDING REVS- CHANGING OF TANKS AND ALSO INSTRUCTIONS FOR GETTING THE WHEELS DOWN BEFORE LANDING AT BOLT HEAD. I.F.F. DISTRESS WAS SWITCHED ON AT 1530 AND THE W/OP TRIED TO CONTACT M/F AND D/F BUT WAS UNABLE TO DO SO. EVENTUALLY THE ENGLISH COAST APPEARED AND AN AERODROME NEAR START POINT FIRED OFF MORTARS AND CALLED ON DARKY FREQUENCY-THE UNDERCARRIAGE WAS LOWERED BY THE EMERGENCY AIR SUPPLY AND WITH NO FLAPS, NO BRAKES AND NO A.S.I. LANDED, OVERSHOT THE RUNWAY, CROSSED A FIELD AND HIT A BRICK WALL. THE A/C SUSTAINED FURTHER DAMAGE AND THE W/OP SGT GUTHRIE BADLY BRUISED HIS HAND. THUS ENDED AN EVENTFUL TRIP WITH A SAFE RETURN WHICH SAYS MUCH FOR THE SKILL OF THE CAPTAIN AND THE HELP OF A WOUNDED ENGINEER. THE A/C HAS BEEN CLASSIFIED CAT B.

Report on Bordeaux raid, 12th August, 1944 from R.A.F. North Killinghome

This report dramatically details the events of this raid and the near crashing of the Lancaster on Bolt Head airfield. The place was one of thirty on this bombing mission escorted by Spitfires. V. Wright recalls that the fuselage was a mass of holes but the plane saw service again after being transported up country and repaired.

Beaufighter Mk II

This kind of plane was frequently seen at Bolt Head and was designed as a night fighter equipped with four canon and six machine guns. It had a crew of two and many were based at Exeter where probably this photograph was taken.

Cottage Hotel Car Park

It is March, 1942, and the camera recalls a mixed group of R.A.F. personnel these being Reg, the Right Hon. Ian Beith, Sgt. Judy Smith, Sgt. Lofty Williams, Corporal Jan Tollery, in charge of "A" watch, and Peter. The photographer is not known.

Spitfire being Refuelled

The distinctive letter E clearly identifies this aircraft but not about what class of Spitfire it belongs to. The Ft. Lt. pilot officer may be awaiting the refuelling of his plane at Bolt Head gaining for moment the attention of possibly a guard dog or someone's mascot.

Pilot's Flying Logbook of Ft./Lieutenant N. P. Gibbs while stationed at Bolt Head, 41 Squadron

Year 1944 Month	Date	Aircraft Type	No	Pilot or 1st Pilot	2nd Pilot	Duty
April	29	Spitfire XII UB	882	Self		Scramble
May	5	Tiger Moth	EB	"		Yeovilton to Bolt Head
May	17	Tiger Moth	EB	"	F/O. Peter Cowell	Bolt Head to Reading
May	18	" "	"	"	F/L. Lord Gisborough	Bolt Head to Fairwood Common
May	19	Spitfire XII MB	881	"		To Bolt Head
May	19	" " MB	843	"		From Bolt Head
May	22	Tiger Moth	EB	"	F/L. Ross Harding	Bolt Head to Upper Heyford
May	24	" "	"	"		Wraighton to Bolt Head
May	27	" "	"	"		Bolt Head to Colerne
May	29	Spitfire XII MB	845	"		Rhubarb. One train and 2 engines damaged
June	12	" " MB	833	"		Rhubarb. Ran out of fuel! Crashed at base
June	17	Tiger Moth DE	374	"		Bolt Head to Roborough
June	19	Spitfire XII MB	875	"		Bolt Head to West Malling

Entries in the Station's Operation Book

7.3.1942: F/Sgt. Kosik of 317 Squadron crashed near Marlborough. He was killed and the plane burnt out.

30.4.1942: Extension of accommodation, new dining room, kitchen and NAAFI and two blister hangars for six planes and two new dispersal sites with huts for ground crew and pilots were built.

1.5.1942: Attacked by five M.E. 190s coming in at a 1,000 ft. at 300 m.p.h. down to 50 ft. dropping two 500 lbs. damaging one Spitfire with one casualty. Four R.A.F. AA Lewis gun posts and one Bren gun were in action firing 304 rounds and one aircraft was seen dropping two bombs on Burgh Island after the Station raid.

15.7.1942: Spitfire crashed into the sea.

11.8.1942: New cookhouse and airmen's mess used for the first time for breakfast.

26.9.1942: Aircraft crashed near Kingsbridge of 133 Squadron. Pilot F/O Beatty slightly injured.

25.4.1943: Station dance farewell party held for S/Ldr. Allen, Station commander.

5.7.1943: At 1800 hours a Tiger Moth of 610 Squadron piloted by Sgt. Roberts force landed in a wheat field near Hope Cove turning over on to its back. No casualties.

29.7.1943: 1 aircraft of 610 Squadron crashed in France. Nothing has been heard of F/O Campbell.

8.8.1943: A plane crashed 5 minutes after take off killing the pilot Sgt. Banff.

12.11.1943: A Dakota en route to R.A.F. St. Mawgan from North Africa landed having lost its way through bad weather.

23.12.1943: Rockets and mortars were fired from the station to indicate position of airfield when an aircraft was circling above in bad weather conditions. A P.R.U. Spitfire, being short of fuel, belly landed in a field near Loddiswell. The pilot, Captain Simon, was unhurt. The R.A.F. Regiment guarded the aircraft. An Oxford flew in and took back the pilot and cameras.

25.3.1944: Spitfire crashed having ran out of fuel and the pilot, F/Sgt. Maynard, was lifted out of the cockpit unconscious and taken to hospital.

10.4.1944: A new control tower was at last operational with VHF and Darky facilities.

12.4.1944: Spitfire of 310 Squadron crashed near the main aerial by the runway. The pilot was F/O Lysicky, the cause being a faulty fuel pipe.

17.4.1944: 17 Spitfires of the Free French 329 Squadron landed. They appeared to be lost, short of fuel; 1 plane crashed on landing piloted by F/Sgt. Lombaert, its under carriage collapsing. Nobody was hurt.

15.5.1944: Air Commodore Pyne of 10 Group overnighted at Bolt Head, took off at 11.44 in a Hurricane and crashed at Dartmouth at 11.51 hitting a balloon cable at 1500 ft. Hurricane fell in flames, completely burnt out on the ground and Air Com. Pyne killed instantly.

23.6.1944: Seventeen Spitfires VII of 131 and 616 Squadron landed as an advanced base for Rhubarb 296.

17.7.1944: Four Spitfires and a Walrus of 276 Squadron carried.

18.8.1944: A Lancaster crashed into the wall below the intelligence office.

23.10.44: Two Spitfires of 310 Squadron based at R.A.F. North Weald were seen overhead running out of fuel and the pilots preparing to bale out. They had returned from a raid on Essen, but saw Bolt Head and landed successfully.

24.12.1944: Warning received of a possible sabotage by German prisoners. Guards were mounted during the night until further notice. 22 personnel stood guard and a Browning gun on the tower was ready to co-operate.

14.3.1945: ENSA variety show in Airmen's mess.

23.3.1945: R.A.F. Gang show visited the station.

15.4.1945: Staff party at Grand View Hotel, Hope Cove.

17.4.1945: Film show in Airmen's mess *Jane Eyre*.

25.4.1945: Official reduction of R.A.F. Bolt Head to a Care and Maintenance basis took place.

27.4.1945: A farewell dance was held at R.A.F. Bolt Head.

30.4.1945: A 2000 hours "C" watch held a party at the Grand View Hotel, Hope Cove.

30.7.1945: The date of the last entry in the Station's Operations Book held in the Public Record Office, London.

Typhoon Aircraft Pilots

No details have come forward about the eight pilots assembled by the wing of this Typhoon fighter, one of many planes that saw action from this small airfield sometimes when a Squadron was based here for just a few weeks and then recalled to other airfields.

Awaiting Orders

Another close view this time showing one of the famous Spitfires, but unfortunately no information about the officer or his Squadron and year. Just an unplanned snapshot of those far off days waiting in the sun of a summer's day.

Courting in the Cockpit!

Whatever this occasion was it does recall some moments of ease on the busy station when R.A.F. and W.A.A.F. came together for a photograph on another Spitfire. Again no details available but just a glimpse of one moment in the life of this small airfield when some of its personnel relaxed.

R.A.F. Form 540

OPERATIONS RECORD BOOK

of (Unit or Formation) R.A.F. Station, Bolt Head, S. Devon.

Page No. 1
No. of pages used for March 1

Place	Date	Time	Summary of Events	References to Appendices
R.A.F. Bolt Head	1.3.43.		Gas Officer P/O Rowland, Armament Officer P/O Walker from Harrowbeer visited the station.	
	3.3.43.		also Education Officer F/Lt. Beattie.	
	4.3.43.		Miss Wakeham NAAFI Welfare Superintendent, A.O.C. A.V.M. Dickson and Wing Commander Ward visited the Station. F/Lt. Abbott 12 Works Squadron.	
	6.3.43.		S/Ldr. the Rev. Fenn and F/O Biddle Accountant Officer.	
	8.3.43.		S/Ldr. Hogg visited the Station.	
	11.3.43.		F/O Manning Equipment Officer, Cypher Officer, Education Officer, -F/Lt.Beattie, Transport Officer Exeter.	
	12.3.43.		S/Ldr. Petrie from Harrowbeer.	
	15.3.43.		Lt. Col. Haigh Liverpool and Scottish visited, also Mr. Glover Section Officer visited this Unit.	
	16.3.43.		Major Gaywood and F/O Puncher, 10 Group M.T. Officer and F/Lt. Andrews visited.	
	17.3.43.		Secretary of the National Trust, Charles Shillitoe, Fairhaven, Salcombe re Air to Ground range.	
	18.3.43.		Wing Commander Ward, and Mr. Cox, (NAAFI).	
	19.3.43.		S/Ldr. Fenn and F/O Biddle from Harrowbeer.	
	25.3.43.		F/Lt. Cuthbert.	
	26.3.43.		S/Ldr. Hogg, F/Lt. Milton, F/Lt Cuthbert from Harrowbeer.	
	28.3.43.		Station visited by C in C. Fighter Command, A.O.C in C. 10 Group. An Air Commodore and Wing Commander of 10 Group. Group Captain Woodhall and Wing Commander Ward. Quarterly muster of S.D's by Cypher Officer Harrowbeer. Found correct.	
	30.3.43.	07.20	Aerodrome attacked by 8 F/W 190's. 1 suspected unexploded bomb 200 yards east of G.C.I. and 40 yards South of G.C.I. Orderly Room. Cannon shell cases found on East-West runway and bomb cases fragments on North of Aerodrome. Advised Duty Intelligence Officer, S/Ldr Rowe. S/Ldr Hogg.	
	"	07.22.	Visited by S/Ldr. Turnbull and F/Lt. Milton to see possibility of accommodating 3 Squadrons under canvas.	

Station Operations Record Book

This is one page from the operations book which provides a day by day record of eve[nts] at R.A.F. Bolt Head from 1941 to 1945. It accurately records all plane movements, visito[rs] to the station, weather conditions and many other interesting facts.

Place	Date	Time	Summary of Events	References to Appendices
Bolt Head	23.7.44.		At 0920 hours F/Lt. Hill and F/Sgt. Cameron of 276 Squadron took off from Bolt Head on A.S.R. patrol. At 09.35 hours after reporting engine trouble F/Lt. Hill dived into the sea 14 miles S.E. of Bolt Head without baling out. His body was recovered dead by an M.G.B. fetched to the spot by F/Sgt. Cameron and transferred to an H.S.L. from Salcombe. F/Lt. Hill had only just taken over command of the 276 detachment on the posting of F/Lt. MacBrian and his loss deeply affected the Squadron. Ramrod 154 was laid on for 611 Squadron and postponed from time to time throughout the day until finally cancelled. One section of two Spitfires IX of 611 Squadron escorted a M.T.B. on special mission from 21.30 hours until last light.	
	24.7.44.		At first light four Spitfires IXa of 611 Squadron carried out a shipping recco of the Channel Islands Granville and St. Malo without incident. At 11.50 hours Ramrod 154 was carried out by 10 Spitfires IXa of 611 Squadron carrying 500 lb. bombs. Direct hits were scored upon the railway line and station buildings at Landiviseau. All our aircraft returned safely. During the later afternoon and evening special convoy patrols were carried out without incident by three sections of two aircraft of 611 Squadron west of Ushant, carrying 90 gallon tanks.	
	25.7.44.		Rhubarb 322 was carried out in two fighter sweeps of 4 Spitfires IX each of 611 Squadron between 1400 hours and 16.20 hours. Roads and railways were swept in Brittany and two locomotives, four lorries and two E/A grounded on Vannes A/F were attacked with cannon and m/g. Throughout the day Spitfires and a Walrus of 276 Squadron made A.S.R. searches off Guernsey without success for a Fortress crew.	
	26.7.44.		Low cloud and mist made operations impossible and there was nothing to report.	
	27.7.44.		Rhubarb 323. 8 Spitfires IXa of 611 Squadron took off at 19.00 hours for a long fighter sweep which penetrated as far as Les Sables and Nantes. Very little activity was seen on road or rail. One 3-ton truck was attacked and damaged near Rennes. All our aircraft returned safely.	

Grand View Hotel, Hope Cove

One of the local hotels requisitioned by the R.A.F. to accommodate WAAF radar operators working at R.A.F. Bolt Tail radar site and at Ground Control Interception (G.C.I.) radar station next to R.A.F. Bolt Head airfield. There was a voluntary run snack and refreshment canteen over the garage to the hotel serving personnel coming off any of the three daily watches.

Enjoying a Summer's Day

Here at the main entrance to Grand View Hotel are men probably from the R.A.F. Police who did duties in the area. They were billeted for a time in the hotel and are here off duty with one of the hotel cooks. One has been recognised as F/Sgt. Isaac and another remembered as a Canadian mechanic.

Shippen Holiday Huts

Yes, even these small wooden huts at Outer Hope were requisitioned by the R.A.F. for accommodating service personnel. They were then owned by Mrs. Peggy Cleave; unfortunately the corporal has not been recognised.

Servicing a Cine Camera
V. H. White is here servicing a cine camera fitted into a Hurricane of 307 Polish Squadron based at Honiton Clyst near Exeter. The G.45 camera was fitted to many planes and operated when the aircraft engaged an enemy. On a few occasions the photographer was flown to R.A.F. Bolt Head to undertake urgent service. The photograph was taken in August, 1941.

R.A.F. Transport
With hundreds of service personnel billeted in the area and many of them working a shift system on the airfield, radar and wireless units transportation was necessary on quite a large and regular scale although sometimes some personnel walk from Hope Cove on a summer's day. Here is a typical lorry probably waiting for a change in shift to take people back to Hope Cove.

Underground Operations Rest Room, R.A.F. Bolt Tail
A rare and probably unauthorised quick photograph of the station's personnel resting during one of the three daily watches. There are sleeping facilities for the radar operations and shelter in the event of an attack.

Farewell to "C" Watch

November, 1943, yet another change in personnel moving from station to station this time by Harry Chaplin who completed six months at Hope Cove in charge of one of the watches. He is here posed for the photographer probably for sending a shot of himself to his family.

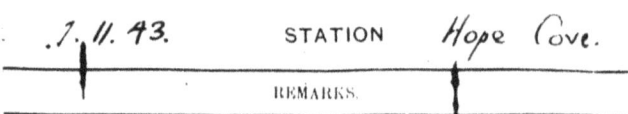

.1.11.43.   STATION   Hope Cove.

REMARKS.

Dear "C" Watch

Give to my successor the same cheerful and efficient service which it has been my privilege to receive from you over the past six months, and then if the poor old hun in his death struggles decides to stick his neck out (beyond Y53 square!!) I know you will clobber him good & proper.

Therefore my best wishes to you as a watch. As individuals my hope for you is, that, when you take up your interrupted vacations or set off on new ones, you will find the comradeship of service life a very real asset.

If you can say "ROGER" and "WILCO" to my aspirations, then I can contentedly but regretfully say. LISTENING OUT.

                 Harry Chaplin

Christmas Menu

In spite of hostilities the 1944 signed menu shows that the festive season was at least enjoyed by R.A.F. personnel off duty at Bolt Head, Hope Cove and Harrowbeer. By this time Allied forces were advancing across France and planes were then able to use airfields formerly used by the Germans and these in South Devon were past their peak use.

Christmas Menu 1944

R.A.F. Stations:
BOLT HEAD, HOPE COVE and HARROWBEER

Breakfast

Cornflakes or Shredded Wheat and Milk.
Bacon and Fried Egg.
Marmalade
Tea or Coffee

Dinner

Tomato Soup
Roast Turkey *and* Roast Pork
Sage and Onion Stuffing. Apple Sauce
Chippolati. Force Meat Balls
Roast Potatoes. Boiled Potatoes
Brussel Sprouts. Cauliflower and White Sauce
Christmas Pudding and Brandy Sauce
Fruit   Mince Pies
Beer or Minerals   Cigarettes
Tea
Cold Ham
Pickles
Russian Salad
Christmas Cake   Fruit Trifle

Wishing you a Merry Christmas and a Happy New Year.

Hope Cove Ground Control Interceptor Radar Station

1. Final Operations Block, permanent brick.
2. Stand-by Power House, permanent brick.
3. Water storage tank and tower, steel.
4. Pump house and well, permanent brick.
5. Sewage Disposal Plant.
6. Ejector Pump House, permanent brick.
7. Latrine, concrete block.
8. Barrack Block, timber.
9. Barrack Hut, timber.
10. Education Hut and Lecture Room, nissen.
11. Barrack Hut and Store, timber.
12. Barrack Hut and Store, timber.
13. No. 1 Interrogator, permanent brick.
14. No. 2 Interrogator, permanent brick.
15. Reserve Aerial plinth, concrete.
16. Final aerial, steel.
17. A.M.E.S. 21, Type 14, concrete.
18. A.M.E.S. 21, Type 15, concrete.
19. Armoury Store.
20. Barrack Huts, concrete.

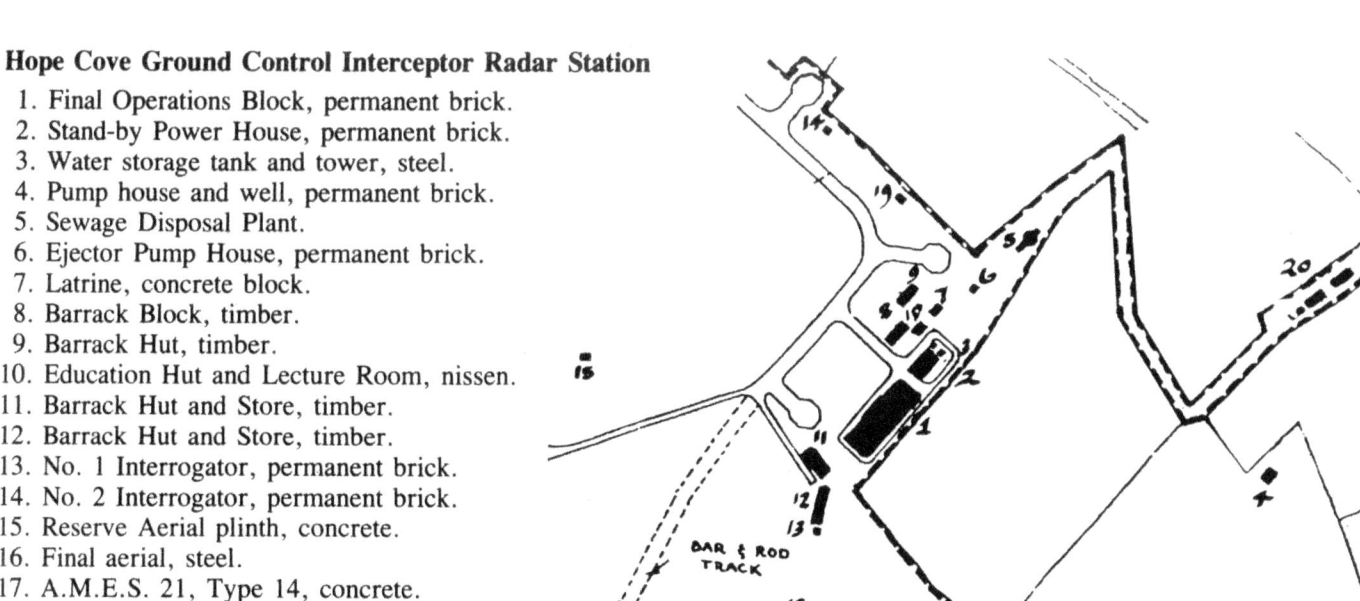

The setting up and development of this G.C.I. radar station right next to R.A.F. Bolt Head airfield was mainly through the initiative and knowledge of Flt. Sgt. Jack Nissen, a young radar technician recruited because of his expert knowledge of the then growing awareness of the role radar could play in the war.

He recalls that he was sent down from London in early 1941 to set up a radar unit in this southernmost area of Devon in early 1941 only to find that his destination, *R.A.F. Hope Cove*, did not actually exist!

However, with thirty or so men they marched from Kingsbridge railway station and eventually found lodgings in Hope Cove. A few days later a two-ton transmitter, a diesel electric generator, aerial trailer and a mobile workshop arrived and they were soon in business. This was sited very close to R.A.F. Bolt Head whose squadrons of aircraft would soon be used to test out the equipment and whose aircraft would eventually rely on this unit and that on Bolberry Down for information on locating enemy planes and as an aid to navigation.

By March 1941 the station started practising for night fighter interception and control by daylight hours. The vehicles were covered over with a camouflage sacking as it was assumed the enemy, who had some knowledge of the chain of radar stations being set up along the whole coastline, would soon attack.

Although of Flt. Sgt. rank only Jack Nissen was the only person who had the technical expertise to undertake this development work and soon many higher ranking visitors would be coming to watch rather anxiously what was going on. It was, of course, top secret, all personnel were sworn to secrecy and pilots from the co-operating planes were not allowed inside of R.A.F. Hope Cove, it being guarded by the R.A.F. Regiment.

Jack Nissen recounts that he and his team had a first class view of the Plymouth blitz with their viewing range up to 60 miles and they were able to plot the enemy aircraft flying to and away from that devastated city.

Planes of the 307 Polish night fighter Squadron co-operated to develop ground control procedures and within a few weeks Spitfires of 317 Squadron operating out of Exeter were also involved. Mesh for the two runways was laid in May, 1941, and practise runs over the Channel and France were undertaken following navigation advice from the radar control room.

It was known at this time that the Germans were also developing a slightly different form of radar detection system and were setting up sites along the French coast one being on the Cherbourg peninsula more or less opposite R.A.F. Hope Cove.

With the entire 317 Squadron moving into R.A.F. Bolt Head, sorties or flights were organised over France using the radar information and pilots were not allowed to use their radios as these may be detected by the German coastal radar sites.

During 1941 the station airfield expanded, nissen huts quickly sprung up, high blast walls covered with turf were built and numbers increased to around 100 personnel.

The co-operation between the radar station and airfield enabled night and day operations by aircraft and from June, 1941, both units were very busy. G.C.I. Hope Cove was continually being modified in these early years of radar use under the ever present guidance of Jack Nissen. By 1942 the *Gee* radar system was coming into use enabling planes to approach targets in France and Germany on an indirect evasive route whereas the German system operated on a single direct route approach to targets in England making their planes a not too difficult target to plot for direction, speed and height and so attack by gun batteries or allied planes.

The *Mandrel* radar jamming system was developed at R.A.F. Hope Cove, Jack Nissen producing a prototype here in Devon which reached its fulfilment in the Normandy landings in 1944.

Like Bolberry Down radar station this one operated an A, B, and C watch around the clock and the original temporary equipment was replaced by permanent buildings, etc. as listed next to the sketch.

Jack Nissen served here from 1941 to 1943 but it was in August, 1942, that he put his advanced radar skills to the test when he volunteered to join *Operation Jubilee*, an attack on German positions in and around Dieppe, France. The object of his mission was to penetrate and evaluate the German *Freya* radar long range radar system operating on the cliffs at Pourville, thought to be the most advanced in use by the enemy.

Off Duty at Inner Hope

WAAF radar operators and probably men who serviced the equipment are grouped here by the wall next to the old lifeboat house. One has been recognised as "Art" the Canadian radar mechanic, readers may possibly fill in names for the others in this carefree group at Inner Hope.

Radar Installation

This wartime photo recalls just what the actual radar installation looked like at Bolt Tail. It was a high power dish transmitter and detector surmounted over the operations room and surrounded by a blast wall. It was referred to as an A.M.E.S. type 52 unit.

By Nissen Hut No. 3

Maintenance personnel at R.A.F. Bolt Tail showing Corporal Russell Smith and Bob Levick with the Canadian emblem. Men were normally billeted on the station or in nearby farmhouses and the WAAFS in Hope Cove.

Billeting

The very large numbers of W.A.A.F., R.A.F. and Army personnel drafted into the area and which was constantly changing meant that almost all the hotels, small guest houses and private houses and farms were either completely requisitioned or they had to take in personnel as and when the need arose.

Many of the R.A.F. personnel were accommodated on camp but, in the main, the W.A.A.F. were at Hope Cove together with officers and some other ranks although it must be emphasised the situation was changing almost from month to month.

Grand View Hotel: Used for W.A.A.F. personnel from R.A.F. Bolt Tail and R.A.F. Police. It was also used for a while as a girls school.

Hope Cove Hotel: This is just above the old lifeboat house and was used by the W.A.A.F.

Greystone Hotel: Also used by the W.A.A.F.

Cottage Hotel: Used by aircrew from R.A.F. Bolt Head with officers and sergeants.

Other small hotels were used, *Cannavilla* and *The Crest*, and *Drakelow House*. Homes were also used in the village.

Hope Cove must have been bustling with service personnel, many coming and going on the round the clock working and extra temporary personnel flying in at R.A.F. Bolt Head.

The village hall was used for a time as a school then for dances by the R.A.F. The Harbour Lights Tea Rooms were also used as a school for London evacuees and even the small wooden chalets near the post office were used for billeting.

Transport was in the form of R.A.F. lorries and these would be working round the clock taking and bringing personnel off their shifts. In a few instances it was said that on a good summer's day or evening personnel walked from Hope Cove to the radar station along the cliff paths.

Finally the old barn above the Methodist Chapel was used as a cinema. Last run by a Mr. Holman people had to bring their own seats for the once or twice a week performance. A small charge was made to cover costs for bringing out from Kingsbridge the projector and screen. Those were the days!

Aircraft Tactics and Codes

Rhubarb: Small attacks on specified targets by sections of fighters under cloud cover, low flying. Mainly a harassing operation.

Intruder: Offensive patrol at night over Hun territory to destroy aircraft and dislocate Hun night-flying organisation by shooting up aircraft and bombing runways.

Circus: Combined fighter and bomber operation on large scale planned to bring enemy fighters into operation. Fighter force then bomber force.

Bomber Force: Bring enemy fighters into action and do material damage to enemy war effort.

Fighters: Fly in a. attack wing, b. escort wing (defends bombers only, closing formation on a Hun attack and maintaining the same angles as bombers), c. escort cover wing (fly at 2,000 ft. above b. to protect, attack and escort).

High Cover: Patrol 8,000 ft. above a. e. target support wing (precede a. by 10 minutes to establish air superiority over target, maintain same angles as bombers, f. forward support wing (follow up bombers and fighters and cover withdrawal of first force. Same height as bombers), g. Rear support wing (follow up f. providing second line of defence), h. free lance (wing of fighters dividing Hun's attention by bombing allotted targets away from target area).

Rodeo: Fighters offensive to destroy Hun's aircraft on the ground.

Ramrod: Fighters escorting bombers to destroy target, fighters only defensive, altitude 5,000 ft. or below.

Mosquito: Small attacks on unspecified targets.

Roadsteads: Fighters escorting bombers diving, low level attacks on Hun shipping at sea or in harbour.

Fighter Roadstead: Fighter or cannon fighters only. Aircraft attack flak ships prior to attack by bombers during which split wing climbs over target and protects them from Hun fighters.

From the notebook of Pamela A. Mills, R.A.F. Hope Cove, 1943.

From the Hope Cove Parish Minute Book

A Committee Meeting held at the Hall on Monday Oct. 5th 1942 at 7.30, 8 members being present.

The R.A.F. had approached the Sec. with regard to running a Canteen for the men and it was decided to run it if rooms were available at Hope, as the Hall was considered too far away.

Mr. Tee was asked to ask Mr. Thornton if he could cut weed around the Hall as last year.

F. Adams, 28.10.42

A Committee Meeting was held at Channel View on Thursday July 23rd at 7 p.m. 7 members being present.

It was suggested that the Hall Committee run a Dance occasionally instead of the R.A.F. running them always, & it agreed to run one every three weeks in turn with the R.A.F., & to discontinue the Whist Drives for August. Dates for Dances

B. G. Fox Aug 4th 1942

The R.A.F. Entertainment Officer had approached the Secretary asking if the Hall and R.A.F. could co-operate with Dances, and film shows, this was rejected by the Committee on the ground that the R.A.F. had given us no previous support, but they may hire the use of the Hall for films at the rate of £1 per night.

D. A. Evans, May 1st 1946

A Committee Meeting was held on May 3rd at 7.45 p.m. 9 members being present.

The Dances for the summer months were discussed, — Mr. Tee proposed & Mrs. F. Adams seconded the R.A.F. & the Bolt Tail W.A.A.F. carry on alternatively with a Dance for the Hall Com, occasionally.

F. Adams, 3.5.43

1 Barrack hut.
2 Barrack hut.
3 Barrack hut.
4 Equipment store.
5 R.A.F. latrine.
6 A.M.E.S. mark VI, nissen hut.
7 R. and T. block, concrete.
8 R.A.F. officers and W.A.A.F. latrines, concrete.
9 Standby set house, concrete.
10 Ablution and fire pool, timber.
11 Admin and S.S.Q., concrete blocks.
12 Technical workshop and M.T. office, concrete blocks.
13 Armoury, concrete blocks.
14 Air raid shelter, pre-cast concrete.
15 Fuel compound, post and wire.
16 Petrol store, concrete blocks.
17 Standby set house, concrete.
18 Incinerator, permanent brick.
19 T. and R. cubicle, permanent brick.
20 Guardroom, concrete blocks.
21 Barrack hut, nissen.
22 Barrack hut, nissen.
23 Barrack hut, nissen.
24 Barrack hut, nissen.
25 Latrine, iron.
26 Ablution block, nissen.
27 Bathroom, timber.
28 Dining and recreation rooms, permanent brick.
29 Fuel compound, post and wire.

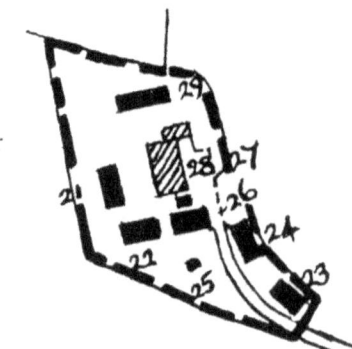

Plans of buildings around the 1909 former Golf Club house.

Plan of buildings close to cliff edge south west to Golf Club house.

This station was designated an A.M.E.S. type 2, 52 unit situated right at the edge of the cliffs on Bolberry Down a hundred or more yards closer to the sea than the present Port Light building originally the club house of a golf course built in 1909 and building number 28 on the sketch plan.

The Air Ministry Experimental Station was one of a chain of units operating along England's southern coast classified as "Chain Home Extra Low" capable of identifying low flying aircraft and surface vessels.

It was built following the construction of the other radar unit, titled *R.A.F. Hope Cove*, situated next to the airfield of *R.A.F. Bolt Tail* about 1½ miles to the east close to Soar Mill Farm in 1941. The type 2, 52 indicates that it was made up of an operations room (see back of cover for general appearance) over which stood a metal gantry carrying the radar dish and mast, all being surrounded by a substantial blast wall.

The larger of the two sketch maps on this page clearly shows the other buildings all surrounded by a fence and guarded by personnel of the R.A.F. Regiment.

A track linked this unit with more buildings which stood around and close to the present Port Light restaurant (dated 1909) these mainly being barracks for accommodation.

The figure 52 shows that it had a high power transmitter used for air and surface watching with an effective 60 miles detection zone that could be viewed on a tube, a planned plotter indicator. All the radar units were linked to nearby important control centres this being R.A.F. Mount Batten for South Devon.

From the plan of the unit all the other small buildings gave support in one way or another to the main ops. room and the unit was protected by a gun site at nearby Bolt Tail.

The station was operational from 1941 until at least the time of the Normandy invasion on 6th June, 1944, after which its role of detecting enemy aircraft and shipping and passing this information on was largely overtaken by events in France.

The radar unit was manned by three watches, A, B and C, for twenty-four hours a day mainly by the W.A.A.F. who were billeted in Hope Cove village and by some R.A.F. personnel billeted in the barracks which stood close to the Port Light restaurant.

Very little remains of this site now except a small area of concrete blocks and brick walls which were blown up just after the war and now partly covered by gorse and vegetation along the top of the steep cliff edge.

This is building number 28 on the above sketch plan built in 1909 as a golf club house and some remains can still be seen of the radar gantry support and concrete building lying just below the cliff top on Bolberry Down.

The work required an expert radar technician but it was made quite clear to him that should he fall into German hands his guard of ten men were to shoot him! The party landed in the early hours of 19th August, 1942, and they encountered unexpected heavy fire. However, for seven hours his group edged their way towards the metal tower and Jack climbed up cutting the eight cables carrying the radar information. Immediately the operators had to revert to radio communications which were picked up by a waiting naval ship.

From the information later decoded much valuable information was gleaned about the current German radar network. Jack did manage to get down to the beach and swim out to a waiting boat but the majority of his guards and many other troops were killed. For this exploit it has been suggested that he be awarded the V.C.

For the rest of the war especially up to June, 1944 the radar station at R.A.F. Hope Cove operated much like its counterpart on Bolberry Down providing valuable information to pilots going out and returning from sorties but also in identifying and plotting the position of incoming enemy aircraft.

Allied planes were quickly scrambled from the adjacent airfield and the pilots instructed to gain a certain height, speed and approach prior to attacking the intruder. This very valuable identification and plotting procedure was one of the main reasons why the Luftwaffe lost the battle in the skies and prepared the way for the 1944 invasion of Europe almost without hindrance from enemy aircraft.

SUMMARY OF INTERCEPTION OPERATIONS AT *Bolt Head* G.C.I. STATION.

Period: from 1800 hrs 26/11/41 to 0800 hrs 27/11/44.

1. OPERATIONS commenced at 1806 hrs 26/11/41 and ended at 2110 hrs 26/11/41 owing to *no further enemy activity in our area*.

2. CREW.

Watch	'B'	'A'	
From ...	18·00 hrs 26/11/41	2300 hrs 26/11/41	......hrs....../......
To ...	23·00 hrs 26/11/41	0800 hrs 27/11/41	......hrs....../......

3. CONTROLLER.

Controller	F/Lt Todd.		
From ...	18·00 hrs 26/11/41	2300 hrs 26/11/41	......hrs....../......
To ...	08·00 hrs 27/11/41	0800 hrs 27/11/41	......hrs....../......
Interceptions:— (a) Attempted	One		
(b) Handed to Fighter ...	One		
(c) Combats	Nil.		

4. WEATHER REPORT FROM SECTOR.

Sunset ......hrs. Sunrise ......hrs.

Moonrise ......hrs. Moonset ......hrs.

Age of moon ....

5. ENEMY ACTIVITY.

Time activity commenced 18·06 hrs 26/11/41 approximately.

Time activity ceased 21·10 hrs 26/11/41.

R.A.F. Bolt Head Ground Control Interception Station

The three daily watches kept records of all operations and weather conditions. This one is for 26-27th November, 1944, reporting two enemy interceptions but no combats. The controller was a F./Lt. Todd.

Living in at Hope Cove

Many of the radar WAAFS were billeted in homes in Inner and Outer Hope in addition to the local hotels. Friendships developed and often they became part of the family as here in Mrs. Jarvis's garden. It was 1944 and Susan Jarvis, her daughter, Betty Carpenter and Mary Ayland make up the group for afternoon tea.

"A" Radar Watch at Bolt Tail

WAAF radar operators enjoying a moment's relaxation these being Brenda Hodgson, corporal of the watch, Barbara Binns, Mary Ayland, Russell Smith, radar mechanic from Canada, Betty Carpenter, Maise Pirie and Mary? Note the heavily sand bagged protection wall.

Enjoying the Sunshine

The summers at Bolt Tail were usually very warm with plenty of sunshine seen here producing smiles for "B" watch off duty against the background of the station. Remembered only as Ivy, Jo, Olivia Parker, Billy, Mitchell, Rene McCall and Doreen readers may well fill in some of the missing names. To whom did the bicycle belong?

From Mrs. F. M. Pilditch, Marlborough:

I had a house at Inner Hope which was my home for 50 years and during the war I had three WAAF "girls" billeted with me. One, Brenda Hodgson, wrote the following poem in 1943. Instead of taking the R.A.F. truck to Bolt Tail Radar Station she would walk the cliff path when weather permitted.

Going on Duty

Tangled in the grass together,
Parched and dry in the hot weather,
Little clumps of thyme and heather
Bend and sway.

And I climb slowly, cap in hand,
To where the radar buildings stand
Waiting on the high headland
Beyond the bay.

Far below me where the rocks rise
The sea stirs, half-asleep, and sighs,
Crystal-green and cool it lies.
I turn away.

Quickly from that sun-starred crater,
I am late and will be later,
And my feet burn for the water
All the way!

From Mrs. Joan Smith (Fry), Canada:

Hope Cove was a wonderful place to be stationed at as a Radar Operator at Bolt Tail. During those years everything was so secretive, and we were sworn to secrecy that the villagers must have wondered what had happened to their peaceful village. They were all so friendly and made us feel so welcome into their homes.

I was at Hope Cove, Bolt Tail, from Feb '44 until the end of the war. We did a great deal of plotting of aircraft and shipping. We worked on a four watch system, 1-6pm, 8-1pm, 11-8am, 6-11pm. There were five or six WAAF or RAF radar operators on duty, and usually two mechanics, who made sure our equipment was in working order. There were times when the enemy dropped "tinsel type strips" to black out our radar screens, and thus sneak in below our beams. We could fairly well detect on our screens, how many aircraft were approaching. We sent these plots to filter room, where they kept track of all our own fighter planes, and could thus identify the aircraft.

From Mrs. Marjorie Bath (Challoner), London:

I was a radar operator in the WAAF during the war and one of the advantages was that postings were usually on the coast.

I had the good luck to spend the years from 1940 to 1943 in S. Devon, first in West Prawle and after a six month break in N. Wales then back to Devon to Kingswear and then to R.A.F. Bolt Tail.

I was billeted in the hotel in Inner Hope and after a short time in its over-crowded quarters, I had the good fortune to be billeted at 'Alberne', with Mrs. Pilditch and have maintained a friendship with her to this day.

It was a wonderful place to be and the village seemed to welcome the guests thrust upon it.

I remember walking along the cliff path one winter night from Inner Hope to Hope Cove where the kind ladies of the two Hopes ran a canteen and where awaited a warm welcome and refreshments.

On that particular evening I looked out to sea and saw a rainbow — only it wasn't a rainbow. It was something I had never seen, a moonbow.

One Spring evening my watch was busy tracking a Flying Fortress which was struggling to reach land. We kept it on our screen until we heard that it had landed on the short runway at Bolt Head and we felt that we had done a good evening's work.

The next morning we went up to Bolt Head and the American crew showed us over the plane and then we watched it lumbering along the runway and finally become airborne much to our relief.

From Len F. Trew, Salcombe:

I first joined my squadron 610 (County of Chester) at Perranporth, Cornwall at the end of 1942, but my operational flying then mainly consisted of convoy protection along the north and south coasts of Cornwall. A very tiring and boring procedure.

In March '43 (or thereabouts) we moved over, lock stock and barrel to Bolt Head, which as you probably know was an advanced landing field comprising two runways formed by laying metal tracking down onto the grass fields, several hedges having been removed to give sufficient length of runway.

The main landing strip ran roughly East to West and with prevailing winds from west/southwest our usual approach to land was from the east coming in over Salcombe estuary towards the cliffs around Stare Hole Bay. A second shorter runway (too short really) ran roughly NE-SW but was only used on rare occasions.

Our squadron was equipped with the clipped wing Spitfire Vb powered by the Rolls Royce Merlin 45 engine, which gave us our maximum speed at low level with a rated altitude (best performance) at about 6-7000 ft.

Squadron Leader Laurie was our CO at the time, and my flight commander was Flt.Lt. Peter Pound. I flew several missions as No. 2 to Peter, and we seemed to get on very well together.

Our operational work still included many hours of convoy protection in the Channel, but we now started to team up with other squadrons based in 10 and 11 Group for wing sorties across to France. Airfields, barracks, troop trains all became our targets, together with close support of bombers raiding a variety of targets from Brest in the far west up to the Calais area.

Operationally we were controlled by "Sector Ops" which I believe was in Exeter, and although CHL radar was in operation then, our main homing assistance when needed came from sector, and comprised the transmission on VHF being picked up by two or if possible three RDF stations who then plotted a position, passed the information to sector who were then able to give us a course to steer for Bolt Head. At least that was the theory.

Life on the ground at Bolt Head was a bit dull, but we found solace in several local pubs where we were made very welcome.

Our officers mess was established at the Cottage Hotel in Hope Cove which made life very pleasant, and the NCO's and others were billeted on the airfield in Nissen huts and in the coast-guard cottages which still exist today, having been transformed into very comfortable homes.

Having completed my operational tour with 610 I left Bolt Head in Jan '43 with a great deal of regret, since I then went north to become a flying instructor.

At Hope Cove 1944
WAAF radar operator Peggy Little is off duty and was one of many hundreds billeted in Hope Cove between 1941 and 1945. She worked at R.A.F. Bolt Tail the A.M.E.S. type 52 station.

At Hope Cove Harbour 1942
Now only remembered as Jack, Dicky, Bill and Midge, the uniformed personnel were a very common sight in the whole area. The quite frequent change of personnel at the stations resulted in many hundreds of people spending part of their wartime duty in this part of Devon when some were here just for a few weeks.

Russell Smith
The date is 5th February, 1945, and he is outside hut no. 3 and was a Canadian trained as a radar mechanic.

A Smart Uniform
L.A.C. Joan Fry off duty and smartly attired in her uniform in February, 1945. She was a radar operator and later married Russell Smith a Canadian radar mechanic.

Other Wartime Activities and Events in the Area

Malborough: An air raid shelter was constructed by placing planks of wood from hedge to hedge in one lane and covered with sand bags. This was occupied most nights by the villagers and some evacuees who came from London for part of the war.

In one of the many enemy aircraft attacks along this coast bombs destroyed one bungalow and there was machine gunning but, fortunately, nobody was injured. The plane went on to Lincombe Farm destroying barns which were later rebuilt.

An American bomber is recalled crashing on the main road to Salcombe just outside the village killing its crew and these may well be the entry in the Kingsbridge mortuary book which records 9 crew were killed on 13th July, 1941, at Malborough.

As there were unexploded bombs on the plane people were warned of the dangers but one person did go into it causing an explosion in which he was blinded.

Bombs fell close to the village one evening damaging the church steeple, the repairs can still be detected, and bringing ceiling plaster down in the canteen then being ran by villagers for local troops in the building now used as a post office (see newspaper article).

Another bomb fell in a lane near Cholwell Farm tearing out a length of hedge on both sides, no one was involved.

South Milton: Three bombs fell late one evening possibly from a raider unloading his bombs on returning to base somewhere in France. One fell in a hedge destroying a greenhouse, another in nearby Sutton and the last in a field by Kerse Road. No one was killed or injured, it was sometime in 1941.

There was also a night raid on the village when a stick of time bombs fell one exploding on impact on the road by the post office. They were all found later buried in fields except one.

Gun sites at Bolt Head: There were three sited at Bolt Head overlooking the cliffs and they became operational in 1941. Bofor and machine guns engaged enemy aircraft on many occasions; they were manned twenty-four hours a day on a three shift system the army personnel living in one of three small asbestos huts on site, the others being used for recreation and cooking.

Hope Cove: A stick of five bombs fell into fields outside of the village during one night in 1941, no one was killed or injured.

Kingsbridge mortuary book: Information recorded for the war years shows the following:
    3rd July, 1943: Plane crash, one killed.
    13th July, 1944: Plane crash at Malborough, nine killed.
    17th July, 1944: Plane crash, three killed.
    25th July, 1944: Plane crash, one killed.
    1st August, 1944: Plane crash, one killed.

Presumably these related to crashes other than those on the airfield at R.A.F. Bolt Head but unfortunately no clues are given about the sites of the crashes or any other details revealed.

Wireless Unit at Pinheys Hill

This high point in the area was requisitioned in 1940 and wooden strut masts of about 90 ft. were erected on a concrete base supporting communication systems. There was also a re-inforced brick and concrete operations room which still stands close to the main Salcombe road. An underground room or shelter was built, the whole unit being enclosed by a large wooden fence.

Farmer J. Rossiter recalled that he rode up to this field on his horse to find military personnel bringing in equipment, a Ford V8 stand by generator, two mobile tenders all without his knowledge although a little later he was handed a requisition notice for this installation.

Like other units in the area it was manned twenty-four hours a day, 10 to 15 personnel were on rotation shifts, these being billeted in nearby farms and houses.

The wireless station was one of many erected along the coast to communicate and co-ordinate messages between stations and aircraft. There was no radar equipment here.

The masts were taken down by Mr. Rossitor, the unit simply being left unused after 1945 and he made good use of the timber and sold off the metal components, this being around 1947/8. One of the concrete bases still stands on the skyline, the other was cleared and the underground room earthed over.

Searchlight Unit at Burleigh Farm

A searchlight unit was set up close to Burleigh farmhouse sometime in 1940 and consisting of one mobile searchlight that could be towed by a lorry. The lighting came from a generator.

Three asbestos temporary buildings were also erected, one for use by officers, another by the non-commissioned ranks and the last as a kind of dormitory come store.

The unit was manned twenty-four hours a day and there were about 10 to 15 R.A.F. personnel involved in a three shift system of working. Mr. Jim Dark, the farmer at Burleigh, said the light seldom came on except when enemy aircraft were close overhead making their way to Kingsbridge. The personnel were billeted in the area.

The searchlight was in place until a little after hostilities had ceased and was probably positioned here to assist in defending any attacks on R.A.F. Bolt Head Station near Soar Mill Farm.

Burleigh farm itself was damaged during the winter of 1943 when a bomb landed nearby in daylight. The blast cracked one wall of the farm but the searchlight unit was not damaged. This isolated bombing may have been caused by the raider releasing unused bombs following a raid in the South Hams. No one was injured.

One of the three wartime buildings still stands and is now being used as a dairy.

SUPREME HEADQUARTERS
ALLIED EXPEDITIONARY FORCE

Soldiers, Sailors and Airmen of the Allied Expeditionary Force!

You are about to embark upon the Great Crusade, toward which we have striven these many months. The eyes of the world are upon you. The hopes and prayers of liberty-loving people everywhere march with you. In company with our brave Allies and brothers-in-arms on other Fronts, you will bring about the destruction of the German war machine, the elimination of Nazi tyranny over the oppressed peoples of Europe, and security for ourselves in a free world.

Your task will not be an easy one. Your enemy is well trained, well equipped and battle-hardened. He will fight savagely.

But this is the year 1944! Much has happened since the Nazi triumphs of 1940-41. The United Nations have inflicted upon the Germans great defeats, in open battle, man-to-man. Our air offensive has seriously reduced their strength in the air and their capacity to wage war on the ground. Our Home Fronts have given us an overwhelming superiority in weapons and munitions of war, and placed at our disposal great reserves of trained fighting men. The tide has turned! The free men of the world are marching together to Victory!

I have full confidence in your courage, devotion to duty and skill in battle. We will accept nothing less than full Victory!

Good Luck! And let us all beseech the blessing of Almighty God upon this great and noble undertaking.

90,000 CUPS OF TEA

Served at Malborough Canteen

The parish of Malborough can well congratulate itself on the various activities which assisted the war effort. Two deserve special mention— the Forces' Canteen and the Wool Party.

From November 30, 1942, when the canteen opened until it closed on July 1 last, more than 90,000 cups of tea and 80,000 meals were served.

This, naturally, meant a great deal of work and it was done by about 40 helpers all of whom gladly gave of their scanty leisure time to make the canteen such a success. There is no doubt that the canteen was greatly appreciated by members of the Forces stationed in Malborough and the surrounding neighbourhod.

Canteen a Boon

Commenting upon the canteen in this month's issue of the Woodleigh Deanery Magazine, the Rev. H. S. Arrowsmith, M.A. (Vicar of Malborough) writes: "Perhaps it is not always realised how dull and lonely life seems to young people who are taken far away from their homes to strange and isolated spots in the country; particularly those whose homes are in big towns. It is to such people that a canteen where they can get refreshments and recreation is such a boon."

Mr. Arrowsmith said a voluntary canteen could not be run efficiently without a good organiser, and they were fortunate in having Mr. L. Edmonds as Secretary of the Committee. From first to last he carried the chief part of the burden of the work upon his shoulders.

The work of the Wool Party, although less noticeable, had been just as valuable. It began when war started under the leadership of Miss Brailsford, who, owing to transport difficulties, had to hand over to Mrs. Arrowsmith at the end of the first year.

Altogether more than 2,700 garments have been made for the Forces and the work is still going on.

All the meetings have been held at the house of Mrs. Thomas.

Cottage Hotel, Hope Cove, March 1942

A general view of part of the village with the Cottage Hotel prominent on the cliffs. A close look at this wartime view of Hope will show a machine gun pillar box in situ by the water's edge and what looks like three large concrete posts standing on the small slipway presumably to obstruct entry from any enemy landings.

Arthur L. Clamp – the man behind the books

Arthur Leslie Clamp was a man of boundless energy with a passion for helping others, particularly through his love of history. A printer by trade, he started his career in a printing company before moving his family from Exeter to Plymouth to teach at the Plymouth College of Art and Design, where he eventually became the Head of the Printing Department.

A Devoted Family Man

Despite his love of teaching, Arthur prioritised his family, always making it home by 5:30pm for tea. He and his wife, Rosemary, raised five children: Susan, Angela, Elizabeth, David, and Steven. Arthur would often combine his love of family and history by taking his children on Sunday walks, encouraging them to appreciate historical monuments by taking photos or making crayon rubbings of gravestones for his books. The family home at 203 Elburton Road was a hub of activity, with a large garden, featuring a two-storey fort and a makeshift swimming pool.

Arthur with his five children.

A Lifelong Learner and Adventurer

Arthur's thirst for knowledge extended beyond history to a deep curiosity about the world. He was passionate about exploring different cultures, traditions, and cuisines, often taking advantage of his long summer holidays as a teacher to travel to places like India, Russia, South America, the middle east and the USA, sometimes bringing one of his children along. This adventurous spirit even influenced his home life, as seen by the short-lived family tradition of steam-cooking vegetables after a trip to Iceland.

History is a prominent feature of family days out

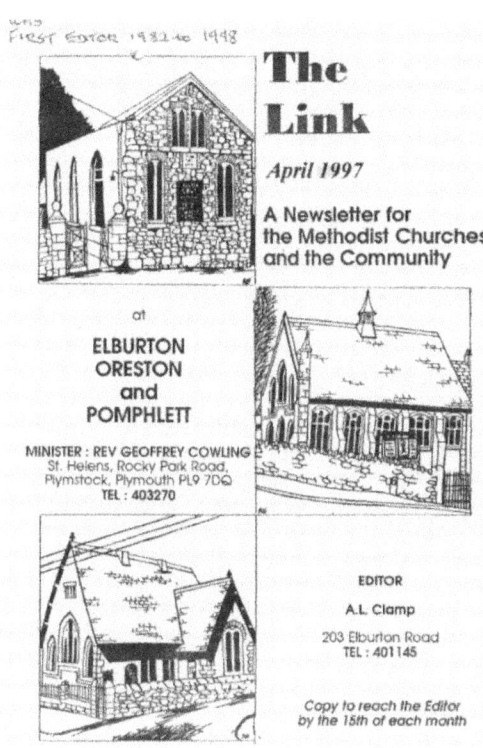

Community and Philanthropic Spirit

His commitment to serving others was evident in his long-standing involvement with the Elburton Methodist Church. He was the Sunday School Superintendent for over 15 years and served as the editor of the wider church's monthly newsletter, "The Link," for a similar duration. After Rosemary's very sad passing, Arthur later remarried and, following a chance encounter with a professor from India, established a connection with a missionary school in Chennai. Together with his new wife, Christine, he co-founded a "Sponsor a Child's Education" program that continues to this day.

Pictured left – The cover of 'The Link' complete with hand drawn sketches of each church by Angela
Below right – Arthur Clamp promoting his latest book
Below left – Arthur at home with his first wife, Rosemary
Below centre – Arthur on holiday with his second wife, Christine

A Legacy of Learning and Positivity

Arthur's greatest passion was history, which he brought to life through tireless research, documentation, and the many books he authored. He was driven by a need to "never be stuck in a rut," constantly seeking new experiences, meeting new people, and expanding his knowledge. With a positive attitude and a great sense of humour, he was always ready to help others, leaving a lasting impact on his family and community. His children, Susan, Angela, Elizabeth, David, and Steven, remember him with love and gratitude.

David Clamp, 2025

A Legacy of Local History

Below is the story of how Arthur L Clamp began writing books, in his own words, drafted shortly before he passed away in 2001. I have only made minor alterations to this text, correcting grammatical errors that he did not survive to correct himself. When I first discovered this text, I was shocked to see my name mentioned. It seems that, unbeknownst to me, I shared my first PC with him. I suspect he used it during the day when I was at school, although I do have one memory of sitting with him and showing him how it worked. It has been a pleasure to pick up where he left off and see his books republished and redistributed, and to know that I was part of the story, even back then. It was also fascinating to discover that his pricing structure matches the way I have tried to price the books, with a third going to local sellers and the rest covering printing costs with a little left over for my expenses.

I am his eldest grandson, and it is a privilege to curate his legacy, which we are calling 'The Clamp Collection'. The very last line of the text originally reads "The following pages list all the titles." Sadly, that page is missing and we have no record of all the books he published and knowing that some of those were researched by other authors makes the process of finding them even harder. I look forward to one day completing the collection and seeing them all available again. And maybe, one day, I'll even start writing my own to add to the series. For now, here is his story in his own words.

Steven Gibson, 2025

Writing and Publishing Booklets on Local Topics and Areas

I started this interest in either 1968 or 1969 when living in Woodford. I had by these dates established the Department of Printing and I think I must have been looking for something different to do. The first titles were of A5 size proofed from type set at Clarke, Doble and Brendon, Ltd., Plymouth printers, and then made up into pages and printed at Sawtell and Neilson, Ltd., Totnes.

Then began a slow process of getting them out to shops, etc. which proved to be more time consuming and difficult than actually researching, writing and getting the books into print. However, I persisted and opened a business account with Barclays Bank on the Broadway. I was advised to give it a title so I called it "Westway Publications". There came along another problem, one of storage of paper and finished books which was solved when the family moved to Elburton in 1970.

I changed the printer to Penwell, Ltd., Callington, Cornwall, as he was then just setting up himself and his prices seemed very reasonable. I did not get any of the printers to make up the complete books. I hand folded the flat printed sheets, stitched the books on a small manual table stitcher and trimmed them in a small hand turned guillotine which I bought from someone in Penzance for £40. It was brought up in a van.

The trouble and time going to and fro to Callington was too much so I transferred the printing to PDS Printers, Prince Rock, Plymouth, and I have been with them ever since. Now they are at Plympton which is easy to reach and they fold the flat sheets which was turning out to be a long chore which only saved a small part of the printing costs.

All my first titles were written by myself. I took the photographs and developed them in the loft of the house, the type was set by now on a computer situated in the house at Elburton from which I had collected photographic lengths of text to cut up and law down as pages.

At some point I decided that I would do my own film processing of lith film so I bought a large second hand process camera from Kingsbridge and learnt through trial and error to make line negatives of the text and halftone negatives of the illustrations which proved more difficult than I anticipated. The main problem was trying to keep the developer in the large dish at the correct temperature as any change would affect the developing time. I replaced this old camera with a brand new one bought from Croydon, Surrey, costing £900. This has turned out to be a great asset cutting out an expensive part of the printer's costs and one crucial aspect of the work which I could control.

By the middle 1970s there were many outlets I had contacted in Plymouth, up to Dartmoor, Exeter, around to Torbay, Totnes, Dartmouth and the South Hams. The market for local books was much greater than I had first thought and through getting to know many local people undertaking research themselves had the chance to help and make up books for other people who had in most instances, got together a collection of photographs with some text in a rather muddled way. Through my experience in print I was able to shape up their work and get it into print and in every case I had to pay the printer and let the person have the royalties. In the majority of titles produced in this manner this was another way of producing titles and it did give some profit to my work. However, I must say that in a few cases I lost out by either the other person getting the numbers wrong, not returning any monies from stock I delivered or they thought that more of their books should have been sold.

The print run was usually 1,000 copies and from time to time I have had reprints of 250 copies. It took about ten years to clear the first print run so I always had large stocks in the garage, workshop, etc. The numbers sold during the early years was about 7,000 copies a year increasing to around 9,000 copies and for the whole of the enterprise about 500,000 have been sold. The booklets have become part of the local scene and many people collect them, shops regularly order copies and I go around certain areas month by month restocking or replacing titles as necessary.

During the past year or so I have started setting the text on a Packard Bell PC, something which I should have done some years back. I share it with Steven Gibson, my grandson. There appears to be no end to the market for local books, but I could not earn a regular income because of the long time it takes to sell stock.

However, now exceeding 100 titles made up mainly of A4 twenty-four page booklets, some folded guides, with selling prices set with a third going to the shop which is the trade custom, the original idea has been quite successful and could go on for ever.

Apart from monetary benefits, however spasmodically these might be, I have learnt a lot myself, met many interesting people and have become part of the local scene with requests to give talks and to advise people about getting into print.

Arthur L Clamp, 2001

This newspaper article, published by the Evening Herald on 17th August 2001, forms a good record of his life. Just as he encourages us to learn more about local history, we encourage you to learn a little about him. For that reason, we have included these pages at the back of all the most recently republished books, in honour of his memory and recognition of his contribution to the community.

www.ingramcontent.com/pod-product-compliance
Lightning Source LLC
Chambersburg PA
CBHW061408070526
44584CB00031B/4192